GRAPHIC MYTHS
EGYPTIAN MYTHS

D0120909

by Gary Jeffrey

illustrated by Romano Felmang

BOOK HOUSE

Designed and produced by
David West 👫 Children's Books
7 Princeton Court
55 Felsham Road
London SW15 1AZ

Editor: Dominique Crowley

Photo credits:
    Page 4 bottom, Trevor Spink
    Page 5 top, Vernon Cheng

First published in 2006 by **Book House,**
an imprint of **The Salariya Book Company Ltd**
25 Marlborough Place, Brighton BN1 1UB

Please visit the Salariya Book Company at:
www.salariya.com

HB ISBN 1 905087 75 6
PB ISBN 1 905087 76 4

Visit our website at **www.book-house.co.uk**
for free electronic versions of:
You Wouldn't Want to Be an Egyptian Mummy!
You Wouldn't Want to Be a Roman Gladiator!
Avoid joining Shackleton's Polar Expedition!

A catalogue record for this book is available from the British Library.

Printed on paper from sustainable forests.

Manufactured in China.

CONTENTS

GODS AND KINGS   **4**

THREE EGYPTIAN MYTHS   **6**

THE STORY OF RA   **8**

OSIRIS AND ISIS   **17**

HORUS FIGHTS SETH   **36**

MORE MYTHICAL CHARACTERS   **44**

GLOSSARY   **46**

FOR MORE INFORMATION   **47**

INDEX and WEB SITES   **48**

GODS AND KINGS

No one knows how Tutankhamun, the eighteen-year-old pharaoh, died.

Ancient Egypt was one of the first great civilisations on Earth. Over the course of 3,500 years, the ancient Egyptians created a rich mythology of stories that expressed their culture, lifestyle and religion.

RISE OF THE PHARAOH

The first Egyptians came from central Africa and settled in the fertile river valley of the Nile. Each year, rains in the south would bring floods to the valleys. The rich silt that settled on the banks made the soil fertile. This allowed the people to farm successfully.

As the civilisation flourished, the country became two separate kingdoms – Upper Egypt in the south and Lower Egypt in the north. Around 3118 BC, Upper Egypt was ruled by King Menes. He conquered Lower Egypt and was the first Egyptian pharaoh to rule the entire land. The pharaohs, who were very powerful, were seen by the Egyptian people as gods on Earth. To honour them, the Egyptians built amazing statues to house their bodies and possessions when they died.

Scientists and historians are still debating how the Egyptians built the pyramids.

ANCIENT TEXTS

The ancient Egyptians wrote down their myths so they could be passed on to future generations. This writing, called hieroglyphics, decorated the walls of pharaohs' tombs. Pyramid Texts were special writings on pharaohs' coffins. They were instructions to guide dead kings through the underworld and gain immortality. Eventually, they were written on papyrus scrolls and collected into a book called *The Book of the Dead*.

Ancient Egyptians used picture symbols called hieroglyphs as a written language.

MYTHICAL MEANINGS

Like other ancient cultures, Egyptians used myths to make sense of their world. Stories about life after death, for example, helped them to understand the yearly renewal of their farmland after the flooding of the Nile. Every year, the land would become dry and lifeless because of the hot Egyptian sun. When the rain came, the soil was renewed and people were able to grow crops. Stories about the world around them gave meaning to Egyptians' lives.

Egyptian gods took many forms. For example, Bastet, goddess of mothers, was often shown as a cat.

This solar disc is a symbol of the sun god. It is used on jewellery and temple doorways from ancient Egypt.

THREE EGYPTIAN MYTHS

The following three stories were famous in ancient Egypt. The first is a creation myth, while the second tells a tale of betrayal and death. In the final myth, there is a fierce battle between good and evil.

THE STORY OF RA

This story comes from the ancient city of Heliopolis in Upper Egypt. Heliopolis was the centre of worship for the sun god, Ra. Ra was one of the first gods. He was greatly admired by the Egyptians.

Ra
Ra, the sun god, is linked to light and heat. His symbol is the solar disc, which he wears on top of the head of a hawk. Ra can change his shape at will.

Thoth
Thoth is Ra's son and the god of wisdom and learning. He wears the head of the ibis (a sacred Egyptian bird). Often, the ibis' head is under a moon-shaped disc.

Apophis
Apophis is the chief demon of the night. He is a deadly serpent who attacks others with mists. His mission is to destroy Ra and prevent the sunrise each morning.

OSIRIS AND ISIS

Osiris was one of the most popular gods in Egypt. He taught people about farming, showing them how to grow crops and live off the land. Egyptians use the myth of Osiris and Isis to explain how they became one of the first great civilisations.

Osiris
Osiris is the first Egyptian ruler who was also a god. He is shown as a green-skinned monarch when dead (page 35).

Isis
As a goddess and the wife of Osiris, Isis symbolises the perfect woman. The ancient Egyptians called her the Great Mother.

Seth
Seth is Osiris' brother and is known as the red god. He has a violent and jealous temper. Seth is associated with the desert and storms.

HORUS FIGHTS SETH

The myth of Horus' fight with Seth takes place over many years. It involves enormous armies and many battles. In this story, Horus battles with the evil desert-god, Seth, to punish him for killing Horus' father, Osiris.

Ra-Herakhti
Ra-Herakhti is an earthly incarnation of Ra. In early mythology he is shown as a king, and is linked to the horizon.

Horus
Isis' son is first seen as a young warrior and then a powerful hawk-headed god. Horus is known as the protector of kings.

Seth
In this book, Seth is at war with Ra for control of the land. He appears in a variety of disguises – including a red hippo.

THE STORY OF RA

FROM DEEP WITHIN THE DARK WATERS OF NUN, A BEING *WILLS* HIMSELF INTO *EXISTENCE.*

UUUUAAAGH!

I AM...

...RA!

PIFFF!

RA FILLS HIS MOUTH WITH WATER. HE SPITS OUT TWO CHILDREN – A BOY NAMED SHU AND A GIRL NAMED TEFNUT.

SPITHOOOOOOOEY!

I WAS ONE GOD. NOW I AM THREE! GO! CHASE AWAY THE DARKNESS AND CHAOS!

SHU AND TEFNUT FLY AWAY, LEAVING RA BEHIND.

NUT GIVES BIRTH TO FIVE MORE GODS.

OSIRIS, THE KING.

HORUS, THE ELDER.

SETH, THE GOD OF STORMS.

ISIS, THE QUEEN.

THESE GODS TAKE THEIR PLACE WITH THE REST OF RA'S CHILDREN – PART OF THE **GREAT ENNEAD**, OR GROUP OF NINE. THEY WILL MAKE ALL FUTURE LIFE, EXCEPT FOR ONE LAST GOD.

NEPHTHYS, GODDESS OF THE HOUSE.

RA CREATES THE VERY LAST GOD – A CLEVER AND POWERFUL SON NAMED **THOTH**.

YOU WILL HAVE THE HEAD OF THE WISE IBIS AND THE POWER OF THE MOON.

RA RISES FROM THE WATERS OF NUN IN HIS SOLAR BOAT. IT IS MADE FROM THE SUN. RA IS READY TO BATHE THE WORLD IN LIGHT. AT THE BEGINNING OF HIS JOURNEY, HE TAKES THE FORM OF **KHEPRI**, THE SCARAB (A TYPE OF BEETLE).

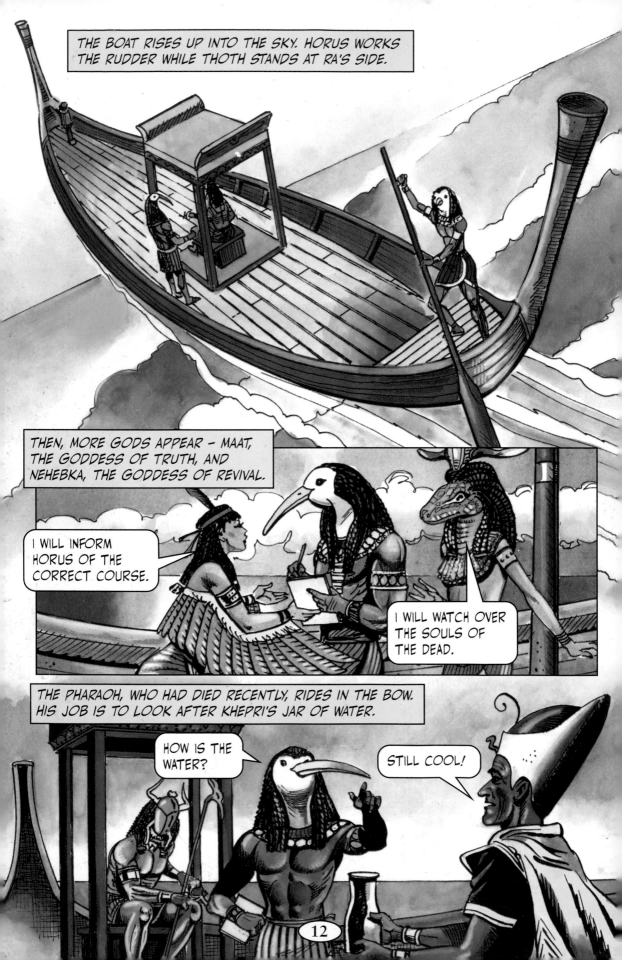

AS THE BOAT CLIMBS UPWARDS, KHEPRI'S RADIANCE GROWS STRONGER.

AT THE HEIGHT OF HIS POWER KHEPRI BECOMES RA – THE SUN GOD.

AS THE DAY WEARS ON, RA'S POWER BEGINS TO FADE. HE CHANGES INTO A HUMAN FORM, CALLED *ATUM*. AS THEY DROP BEHIND THE WESTERN MOUNTAINS, THEY PREPARE TO ENTER...

...*TUAT*, THE UNDERWORLD.

THE DARK KINGDOM IS APPROACHING FAST!

FEAR NOT! WE ARE READY FOR **THEM**.

THEM: THE LEGION OF DEVILS THAT SPRANG FROM THE DARKNESS.
BEWARE! THE GREAT SNAKE LEADS THE CHARGE!
HIISSSSSSSSSSSS!
WATCH OUT! HE SPRAYS BLACK MIST!!!
WE CAN'T DEFEAT HIM!!
THE SERPENT'S NAME IS APOPHIS. THIS FIERCE NIGHT-DEMON ATTACKS THE BOAT...
ATUM STEPS IN.
PHWUMMM!
FEEL THE POWER OF MY DEADLY SUNBEAMS!

OSIRIS AND ISIS

IN ANCIENT TIMES, EGYPT WAS A WILD AND DANGEROUS PLACE. PEOPLE WOULD TEAR EACH OTHER APART AND RIP BODIES LIMB FROM LIMB TO FEAST ON **HUMAN FLESH!**

GRRRAAAAGH!

THEN, ONE DAY, OSIRIS WAS BORN.

BEHOLD! THE LORD OF ALL THINGS COMES FORTH INTO THE LIGHT!

OSIRIS, BORN OF THE GODDESS NUT, BECOMES THE FIRST KING OF EGYPT. HE TEACHES THE PEOPLE HOW TO FARM THE LAND, HONOUR THE GODS, AND OBEY HIS FAIR LAWS.

EVENTUALLY, OSIRIS RETURNS TO EGYPT IN TRIUMPH.

TONIGHT IT SHALL BEGIN!

LATER, WHEN THE PALACE IS QUIET, SETH CREEPS INTO THE KING'S BED CHAMBER.

AS OSIRIS SLEEPS, SETH CAREFULLY MEASURES HIS BODY.

...MAY KEEP IT FOREVER!

ONE BY ONE, THE GUESTS TRY THE COFFIN FOR SIZE.

TOO TALL!

TOO SMALL!

THEY ALL FAIL TO FIT.

SOON ONLY OSIRIS IS LEFT...

YOUR MAJESTY, WOULD YOU LIKE TO TRY?

OSIRIS TRIES THE COFFIN.

EARLIER, AT THE PALACE, ISIS WAS WITH HORUS, HER SON, IN HER CHAMBER WHEN...

GASP! OSIRIS' SOUL IS LIFTING FROM HIS BODY. MY HUSBAND IS DEAD!

ISIS TAKES HER SON AND FLEES TO THE FLOATING ISLAND CITY OF PÉ, IN THE MARSHES OF THE NILE DELTA.

SHE SEEKS OUT THE GODDESS UAZET AT THE TEMPLE OF WADJET.

TAKE LITTLE HORUS. SHELTER AND PROTECT HIM.

24

ISIS WANDERS THE LAND. SHE ASKS THE CHILDREN IF THEY HAVE SEEN OSIRIS. THEY TELL HER THE PATH SHE SHOULD TAKE.

SHE FOLLOWS THE TRAIL. EVENTUALLY, IT LEADS HER TO THE COAST OF BYBLOS.

ISIS RESTS BY THE DESERTED SHORE.

THEN...

HELLO!

HELLO!

WHO ARE YOU?

I AM ISIS. WHO ARE YOU?

WE ARE LADIES IN WAITING...

...FOR THE QUEEN OF BYBLOS!

THIS IS WHERE WE COME TO BATHE.

THE MAIDENS SIT WITH ISIS AND ALLOW HER TO PLAIT THEIR HAIR. THE WHOLE TIME, SHE BREATHES A SWEET SCENT ON THEM.

WHEN THEY RETURN TO THE PALACE, THEY ARE MET BY QUEEN ATHENIS.

WHAT IS THAT WONDERFUL SMELL?

IT'S FROM THE SAD LADY WHO WAITS BY THE SHORE.

ATHENIS CALLS ISIS TO THE PALACE.

WHY ARE YOU SO SAD?

I MISS MY SON, HORUS.

I HAVE A SON, TOO, BUT HE IS SICK.

COME! YOU MUST TAKE ME TO HIM!

THE PRINCE'S NAME IS DIKTYS.

I FEAR MY POOR ANGEL IS DYING!

I CAN HEAL HIM, BUT YOU MUST GIVE HIM OVER TO MY CARE.

AND WHATEVER HAPPENS YOU MUST NOT INTERRUPT ME.

THE QUEEN AGREES.

ATHENIS KEEPS HER DISTANCE. THE DAYS PASS AND, SLOWLY, A CHANGE COMES OVER DIKTYS.

SHE'S MAKING HIM WELL, BUT HOW? I WILL ASK MY SERVANTS.

EVERY NIGHT SHE LOCKS US OUT....

...SHE MAKES A BIG FIRE...

...AND THEN WE HEAR NOTHING BUT THE SOUND OF A SWALLOW!

I MUST FIND OUT WHAT SHE'S DOING.

KING MALKANDER ORDERS THAT THE PILLAR BE CUT OPEN.

THWAK!

SPLINTER!

OSIRIS, MY LOVE!

HAVING REMOVED OSIRIS' BODY, THE PILLAR IS TAKEN DOWN AND WRAPPED IN FINE LINEN. ISIS SPRINKLES SWEET SPICES AND BLOSSOMS ON IT AND RETURNS IT TO THE ROYAL COUPLE.

THIS TIME, ISIS SETS OUT IN A PAPYRUS BOAT. SHE IS HELPED BY ALL THE ANIMALS OF THE WILD.

EACH TIME SHE FINDS A PIECE OF OSIRIS' BODY, ISIS PRETENDS TO BURY IT. SHE MAKES A SHRINE TO MARK THE PLACE.

THIS IS DONE TO **DECEIVE** SETH WHILE SHE SECRETLY PIECES OSIRIS BACK TOGETHER AGAIN.

HUSBAND, I HAVE MADE YOU **WHOLE** BUT I CANNOT MAKE YOU **LIVE**. ONLY OUR VENGEANCE CAN DO THAT.

UNTIL THEN, OSIRIS CONTINUES TO RULE IN TUAT, *THE KINGDOM OF THE DEAD.*

THE END

Horus Fights Seth

DURING THE 363RD YEAR OF HIS REIGN ON EARTH, THE GOD RA-HERAKHTI BRINGS HIS ARMY TO NUBIA FOR A MAJOR BATTLE AGAINST THE EVIL GOD, SETH.

TODAY COULD BE OUR DAY FOR VICTORY. ARE YOU READY, HORUS?

AS YOU KNOW, I WOULD GIVE A **DAY** OF FEASTING FOR JUST ONE HOUR OF FIGHTING!

THE YOUNG GOD, HORUS, IS ONE OF RA'S MOST EAGER LIEUTENANTS.

AND WHAT WOULD YOU GIVE FOR THE CHANCE TO AVENGE YOUR FATHER?

ANYTHING!

SETH HAD KILLED HORUS' FATHER, OSIRIS, YEARS BEFORE. HIS MOTHER, ISIS, HAD SWORN HER SON WOULD SEEK VENGEANCE.

SUDDENLY, SETH'S MEN CANNOT RECOGNISE ONE ANOTHER.

THOUGH THEY SHOUT, THEY ARE UNABLE TO UNDERSTAND EACH OTHER'S WORDS.

THINKING THE ENEMY IS AMONG THEM, THEY *PANIC* AND START ATTACKING EACH OTHER.

WHILE THE SOLDIERS OF SETH'S ADVANCE GUARD KILL EACH OTHER, RA'S ARMY RUSH FORWARD. MEANWHILE, HORUS IS SEEKING *SETH.*

WHERE ARE YOU? WHERE ARE YOU?

THERE! AT THE REAR!

AS THE TWO SIDES MEET, HORUS DIVES IN.

RED GOD! YOUR TIME ON EARTH IS NEARLY OVER!

OOOOFF!

GRAAAGH! I HAVE YOU!

THIS IS FOR MY MOTHER!

THAK!

HORUS CUTS HIS ENEMY'S BODY INTO FOURTEEN PIECES.

THEN...

HORUS, LOOK!!! IT'S NOT SETH!

AND THIS IS FOR MY FATHER!

I MUST FIND HIM!

BUT THEY WILL NOT DUEL TOGETHER UNTIL MANY YEARS LATER...

MORE MYTHICAL CHARACTERS

Egyptian myths feature many other gods apart from the Great Nine. Here is a selection of other important gods and goddesses.

AMUN — Amun is the god of the wind. Usually, he is shown wearing a crown with two large feathers in it. Amun becomes very important when joined to Ra. As Amun-Ra he is the supreme god of Egypt.

ANUBIS — Anubis is associated with funerals and mummies. He has the head of a jackal. Anubis was the first to cover the dead in a protective liquid that kept the bodies fresh. This is a process called embalming. He also guards the dead in their tombs.

BES — This fat little dwarf is known as the god of dance, music and pleasure. His job is to make children happy. He is often shown with a curly beard.

HATHOR — An important goddess of love and fertility, Hathor is often shown as a cow, or sometimes as a woman wearing a head-dress. She becomes Sakhmet, goddess of war and destiny, after Ra sends her to destroy people on Earth.

KHNUM — Khnum is a creator god whose name means 'the moulder'. Usually, he is drawn with a human head and sheep's body, making people on a potter's wheel. He is believed to be a protector of the river Nile.

KHONSU — The god of the moon and time, Khonsu is thought to have magical powers that could drive out evil spirits from humans. Many works of Egyptian art show him as a mummy with a curved moon resting above his head.

MONTU — Montu is linked to winning wars. He is close friends with Amun and, later becomes his adopted son. Montu is often shown with a hawk's head. He has a sacred bull, which is believed to be the soul of Ra.

MUT — Mut is the mother-goddess of all other goddesses. She wears either a vulture head-dress, or a lion head-dress. Mut is married to Amun-Ra and is the queen of heaven.

PTAH — This god is thought to be the designer of the universe. He holds a sceptre, and is shown as a mummy. Everything on Earth is thought to have been made by him. Ptah is so important that some people believe that other gods are Ptah in a different form. Some small communities, such as the one at Memphis, also saw him as the god of artists.

SAKHMET — A close friend of Ptah, she is the goddess of war and battles. She begins life as Hathor, but changes to Sakhmet when she destroys all of Ra's enemies. Her name means 'the powerful one'. She is seen as a woman with the head of a lioness.

SHU — This god of the air is one of a pair of gods who hold up the sky above Earth. He is often shown with an ostrich feather on his head.

SOBEK — Sobek is known as the crocodile god because of his appearance. He is the god of fertility, both of people and their crops. He is also associated with water.

TEFNUT — Tefnut is the twin sister of Shu. She holds the sky above Earth with him. She has the head of a lioness. In early stories, she is the goddess of the moon. In later tales, she is the goddess of dew and rain.

WADJET — This goddess keeps Lower Egypt safe. Wadjet is shown as a cobra. She has wings and a red crown. At other times, she is seen as a woman wearing a red crown and holding a sceptre.

GLOSSARY

advance guard A group of soldiers who travel ahead of the main group of soldiers in an army.

avenge To take satisfaction in punishing a wrongdoer.

awe To feel a great sense of wonder at something.

chaos A state of total confusion where there is no order or control.

deceive To be false or lie on purpose.

delta The place where a river meets the sea.

duel A fight between two people.

eclipse When a moon, a star or a planet hides all or part of another.

epic A very long poem about a hero.

eternal When something will last forever.

fertile Land that produces many plants or crops.

flourish To grow and be successful.

harpoon Sharp spear used to kill animals.

hieroglyphics A type of Egyptian writing that uses pictures and symbols (hieroglyphs) instead of words.

incarnation When a god appears in human form.

inform To give someone knowledge.

linen Light woven fabric, usually made from the flax plant.

mortal A being who will die eventually. Humans are mortal, but gods are immortal because they live forever.

papyrus A type of paper made from the papyrus plant.

reign The period of time that a person, such as a king or queen, rules a country.

rouse To wake up.

rudder A flat piece of wood attached to the back of a boat. When the rudder is turned, the boat changes direction.

silt A type of mud that has lots of food for plants in it.

swallow A small bird that has a short beak and long pointed wings. It catches insects to eat while it is flying.

tamarisk tree A shrub or small tree, with feathery leaves and pink or white blossom, found in the Mediterranean and central Asia.

thicket A thick group of plants or bushes.

tragedy A very sad story in which the main character dies.

underworld The place where souls go after bodies have died.

FOR MORE INFORMATION

ORGANISATIONS

The British Museum
Great Russell Street
London, WC1B 3DG
www.thebritishmuseum.ac.uk

The Egypt Centre
University of Wales Swansea
Singleton Park,
Swansea, SA2 8PP

The Ashmolean Museum
Beaumont Street
Oxford, OX1 2PH

FOR FURTHER READING
If you liked this book, you might also want to try:

Cleopatra: The Life of an Egyptian Queen
by Gary Jeffrey and Kate Petty, Book House 2005

How to be an Ancient Egyptian Princess
by Jacqueline Morley, Book House 2005

Avoid becoming an Egyptian Pyramid Builder!
by Jacqueline Morley, Book House 2004

Inside the Tomb of Tutankhamun
by Jacqueline Morley, Book House 2005

INDEX

A

Apophis, 6, 14, 15, 16
Atum, 13, 14, 16

B

Book of the Dead, The, 5
Byblos, 23, 25, 26

C

coffin, 5, 21-23, 32
creation, 4, 5, 6, 9, 10, 11, 44

E

Ennead, 11
Ethiopia, 18

G

goddesses, 7, 11, 12, 17, 24, 18, 44-45
gods, 4-11, 17, 30, 34, 36, 38, 43, 44-45
Greeks, 5, 7

H

Heliopolis, 6
hieroglyphics, 5
Horus the Elder, 7, 11, 12, 15
Horus the Younger, 18, 22, 24, 27, 32, 34, 36-38, 40, 41, 43

I

Illiad, The, 7
Isis, 7-9, 11, 17, 18, 24-27, 29-32, 34-36

K

kings, 4, 5, 6, 7, 9, 17, 19, 20, 25, 30-32

L

Lower Egypt, 4, 45

N

Nun, 6, 8, 11

O

Osiris, 6-8, 11, 17-20 21-26, 31-36, 43

P

papyrus, 5, 35
pharaoh, 4, 5, 12
pyramids, 4, 5

R

Ra, 6-8, 13, 44, 45
Ra-Herakhti, 7
river Nile, 4, 5, 23, 34, 44

S

Seth, 7, 36
snakes, serpents, 6, 14, 16, 45
solar boat, 11
solar discs, 6, 37
sun, 5, 6, 9, 13

T

Thoth, 6, 11, 12
Tutankhamun, 4

U

underworld (Tuat), 13, 35
Upper Egypt, 4, 6

Web Sites

Due to the changing nature of Internet links, the Salariya Book Company has developed an online list of Web sites related to the subject of this book. This site is updated regularly. Please use this link to access the list:

http://www.book-house.co.uk/gmyth/egypt